This Book Is Given

To:

_____

From:

_____

Claim your FREE gift! Visit: www.amillionseeds.com

Nihil Obstat: Monsignor Douglas J. Mathers, JCD
                             Vice Chancellor

Imprimatur: +Timothy Michael Cardinal Dolan
                             Archbishop of New York
                             May 12, 2022

    The *Nihil Obstat* and *Imprimatur* are an official declaration by competent ecclesiastical authority that the book is free from doctrinal error and contains nothing contrary to Catholic faith or morals. It does not imply that those granting the *Nihil Obstat* and *Imprimatur* agree with the contents, statements, or opinions expressed in the work.

A Million Seeds Inc. provides special discounts when purchased in larger volumes for promotional purposes, as well as for fundraising and educational use. For more information, please email: Jane@amillionseeds.com

"Mysteries of the Holy Rosary, The Life of Jesus and Mary"
First edition 2022 Copyright With Love From Above Books, Inc. 2022
All rights reserved. No part of this publication may be produced, stored in a retrieval system or transmitted in any form or by any means, electronic, mechanical, photocopying, recording, or otherwise without written permission of the publisher.

Edited by Glenys Nellist.
Library of congress Control Number: 2022934355

ISBN paperback: 978-1-7379652-6-8

ISBN hardback: 978-1-7379652-7-5

ISBN e-book: 978-1-7379652-8-2

This book is dedicated to my mom, Rena, who taught me how to pray the Holy Rosary with the mysteries; to my dad, Alfonso, who prayed the rosary even if he didn't have rosary beads, because he had ten fingers to count the Hail Marys; and to my grandsons, Levi and Milo, who inspire me to educate children about the love and sacrifice of Jesus and Mary. I look forward to sharing this book with them and teaching them the Holy Rosary. - Jane Morrone

To Shay and Landon: Whose love for Jesus has brought me closer to His teachings.

–Heather Lean

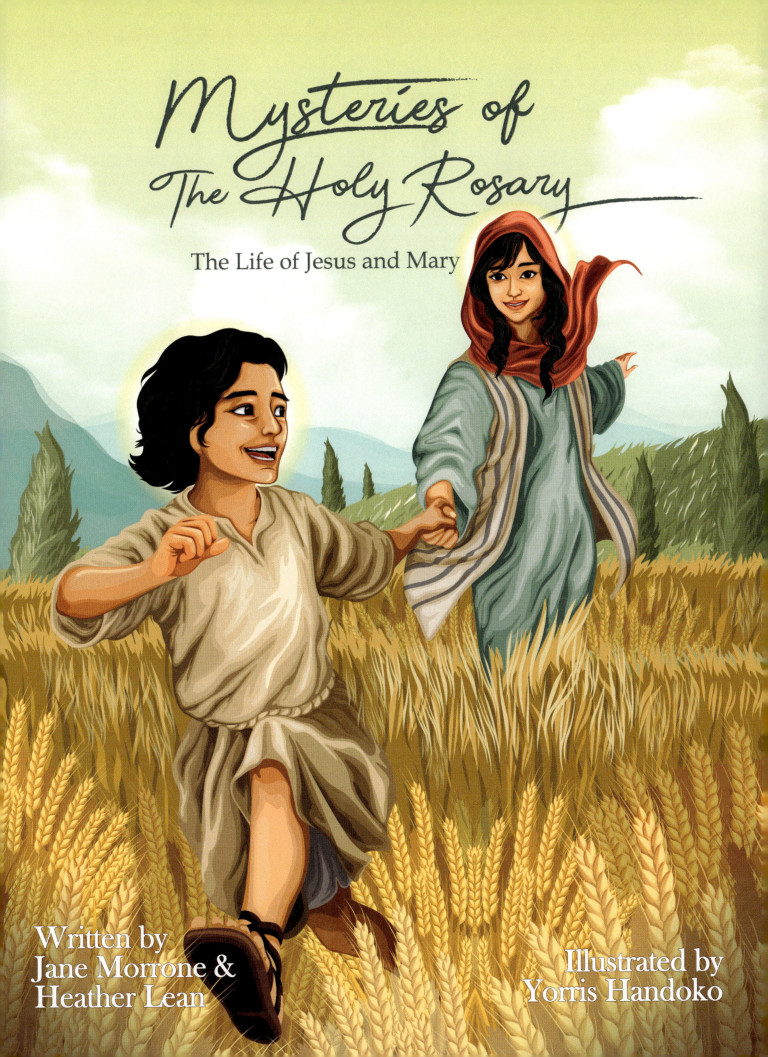

How to Pray The Rosary

1. Begin by holding the Crucifix and saying the Sign of the Cross and The Apostles' Creed.

2. On the first bead, say one Our Father.

3. Say one Hail Mary on each of the next three beads.

4. Say one Glory Be to the Father.

5. At the beginning of each decade, announce the Mystery to be contemplated. For example, the first Joyful Mystery is The Annunciation. After a short pause for reflection, say one Our Father on the large bead.

6. Say ten Hail Marys on the ten smaller beads, followed by one Glory Be to the Father and the Fatima Prayer.

7. Say the second mystery and continue in the same manner until each of the five mysteries of the selected group are said.

8. Conclude by saying Hail Holy Queen, closing prayers, and the Sign of the Cross.

The Joyful Mysteries
(Monday, Saturday and Sundays of Advent and Christmas)

1) The Annunciation
2) The Visitation
3) The Birth of Jesus
4) The Presentation at the Temple
5) The Finding of Jesus in the Temple

The Luminous Mysteries
(Thursday)

1) The Baptism of Jesus
2) The Wedding Feast at Cana
3) The Proclamation of the Kingdom
4) The Transfiguration
5) The Institution of the Eucharist

The Sorrowful Mysteries
(Tuesday, Friday and Sundays during Lent)

1) The Agony in the Garden
2) The Scourging at the Pillar
3) The Crowning with Thorns
4) The Carrying of the Cross
5) The Crucifixion

The Glorious Mysteries
(Wednesday and Sunday)

1) The Resurrection of Jesus
2) The Ascension of Jesus into Heaven
3) The Descent of the Holy Spirit
4) The Assumption of Mary into Heaven
5) The Coronation of Mary

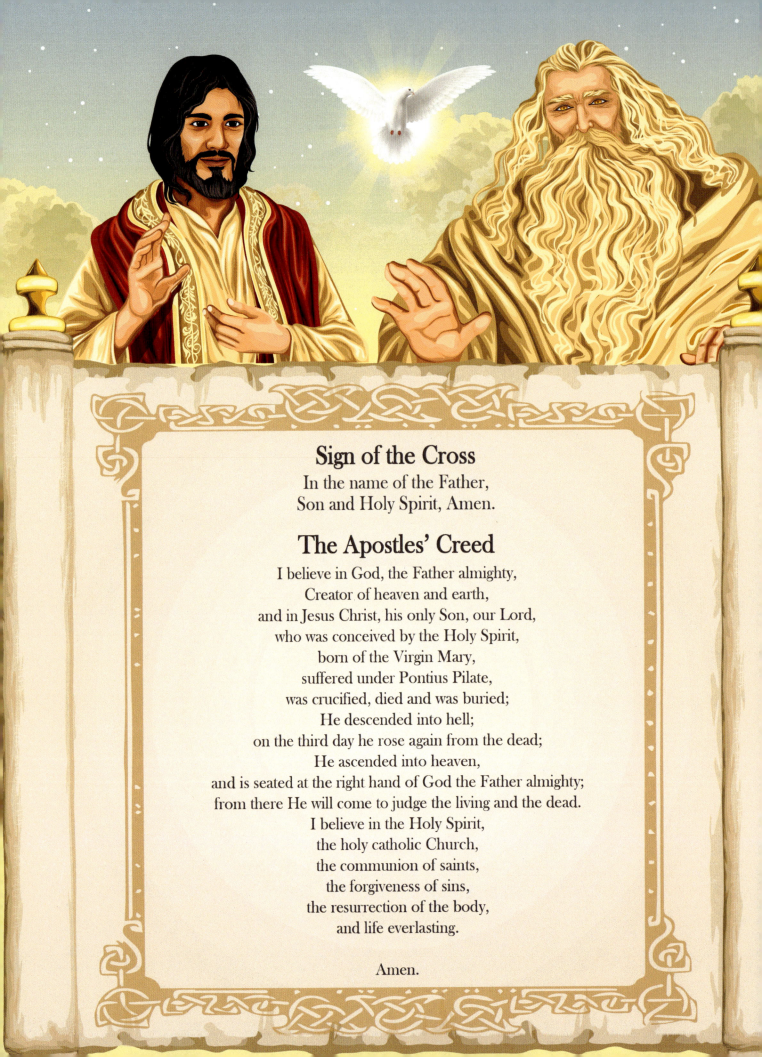

Sign of the Cross

In the name of the Father,
Son and Holy Spirit, Amen.

The Apostles' Creed

I believe in God, the Father almighty,
Creator of heaven and earth,
and in Jesus Christ, his only Son, our Lord,
who was conceived by the Holy Spirit,
born of the Virgin Mary,
suffered under Pontius Pilate,
was crucified, died and was buried;
He descended into hell;
on the third day he rose again from the dead;
He ascended into heaven,
and is seated at the right hand of God the Father almighty;
from there He will come to judge the living and the dead.
I believe in the Holy Spirit,
the holy catholic Church,
the communion of saints,
the forgiveness of sins,
the resurrection of the body,
and life everlasting.

Amen.

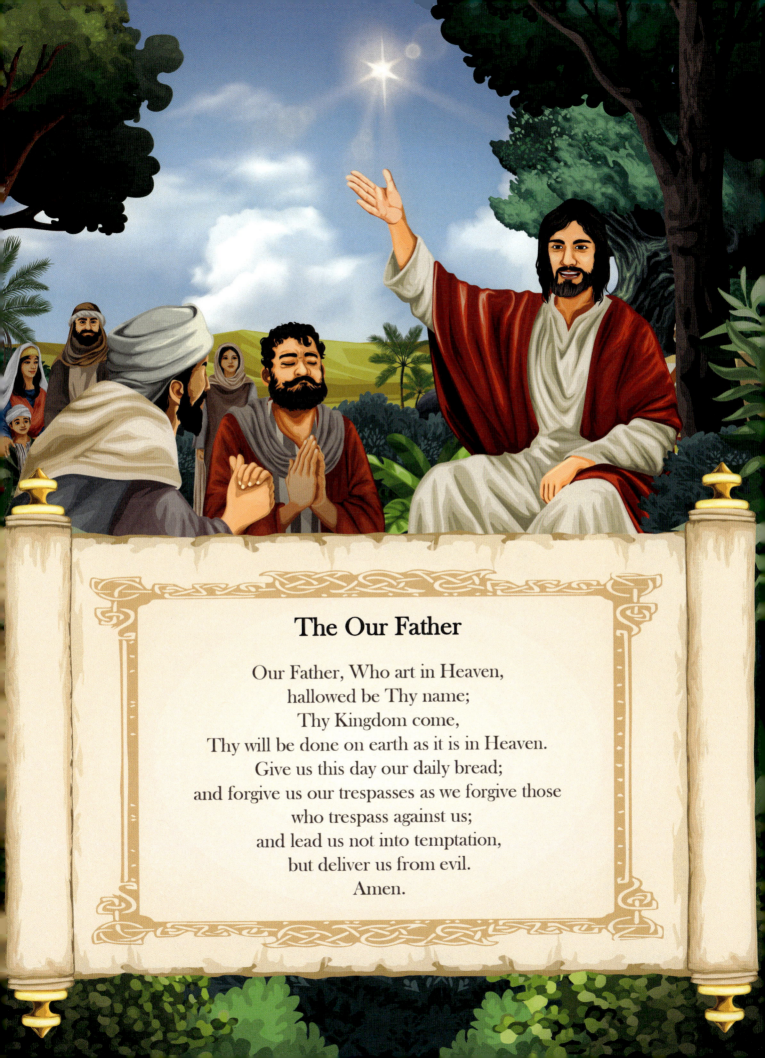

The Our Father

Our Father, Who art in Heaven,
hallowed be Thy name;
Thy Kingdom come,
Thy will be done on earth as it is in Heaven.
Give us this day our daily bread;
and forgive us our trespasses as we forgive those
who trespass against us;
and lead us not into temptation,
but deliver us from evil.
Amen.

The Hail Mary

Hail, Mary, full of grace,
the Lord is with thee.
Blessed art thou amongst women
and blessed is the fruit of thy womb, Jesus.
Holy Mary, Mother of God,
pray for us sinners,
now and at the hour of our death.
Amen.

The Glory Be

Glory be to the Father
and the Son
and to the Holy Spirit
as it was in the beginning
is now and ever shall be
world without end.
Amen.

The Fatima Prayer

O my Jesus, forgive us our sins,
save us from the fires of hell,
and lead all souls to Heaven,
especially those in most need of
Thy mercy.
Amen.

The Hail Holy Queen

Hail, Holy Queen, Mother of Mercy,
our life, our sweetness and our hope.
To thee do we cry,
poor banished children of Eve.
To thee do we send up our sighs,
mourning and weeping in this valley of tears.
Turn then, O most gracious advocate,
thine eyes of mercy toward us,
and after this our exile
show unto us
the blessed fruit of thy womb, Jesus.
O clement, O loving,
O sweet Virgin Mary.

Closing Prayers

O God, whose only-begotten Son,
by His life, death and resurrection,
has purchased for us the rewards of eternal life;
grant, we beseech Thee, that, meditating upon
these mysteries of the Most Holy Rosary of
the Blessed Virgin Mary, we may imitate
what they contain and obtain what they promise,
through the same Christ our Lord, Amen.

May the divine assistance remain always with us.

And may the souls of the faithful departed,
through the mercy of God, rest in peace.
Amen.

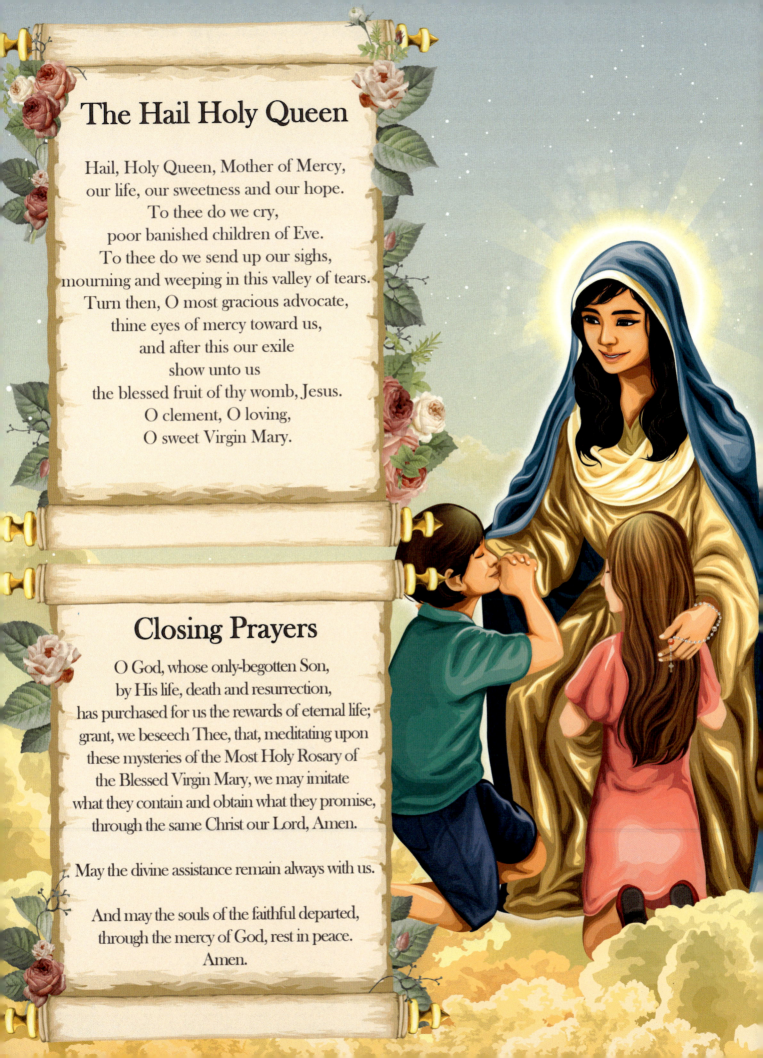

The Joyful Mysteries
(Monday, Saturday and Sundays of Advent and Christmas)

1) The Annunciation
2) The Visitation
3) The Birth of Jesus
4) The Presentation at the Temple
5) The Finding of Jesus in the Temple

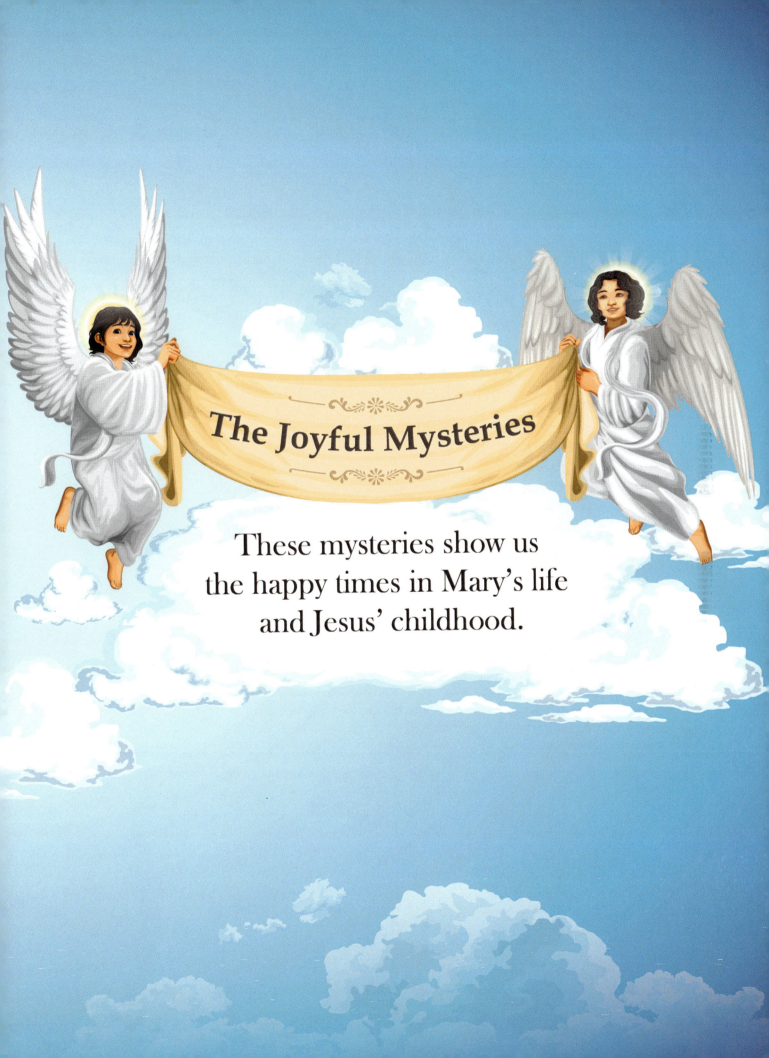

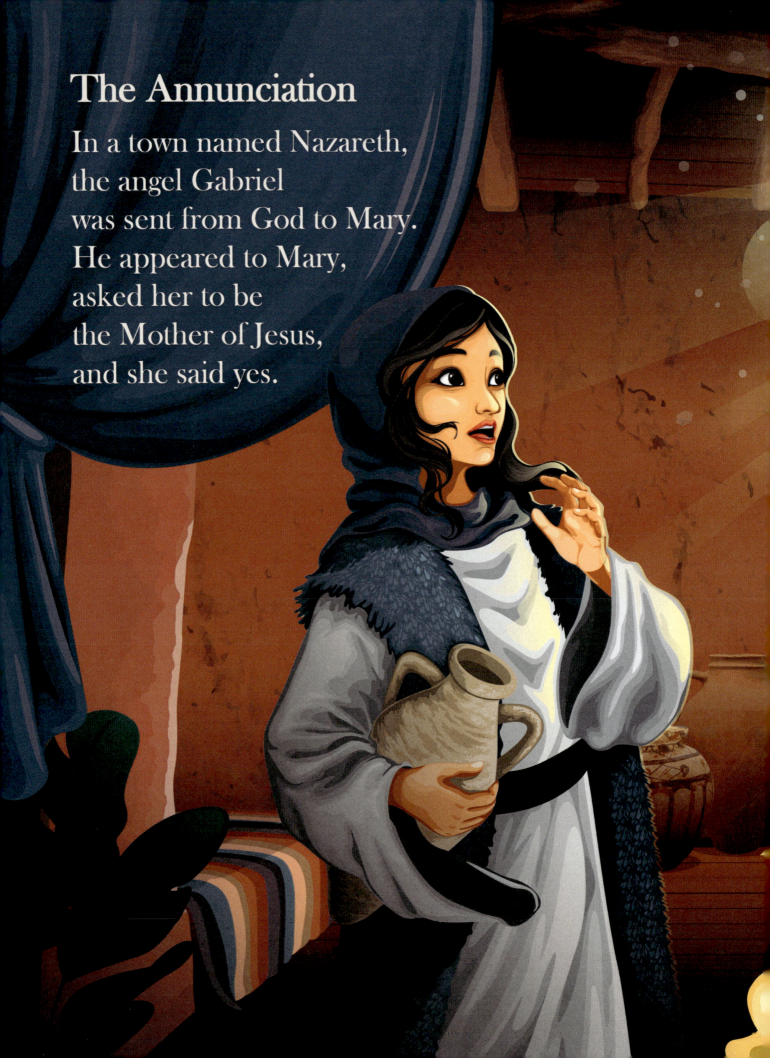

The Annunciation

In a town named Nazareth, the angel Gabriel was sent from God to Mary. He appeared to Mary, asked her to be the Mother of Jesus, and she said yes.

The Visitation

Mary visits her cousin, Elizabeth. The baby in Elizabeth's womb, John the Baptist, jumps for joy when they meet.

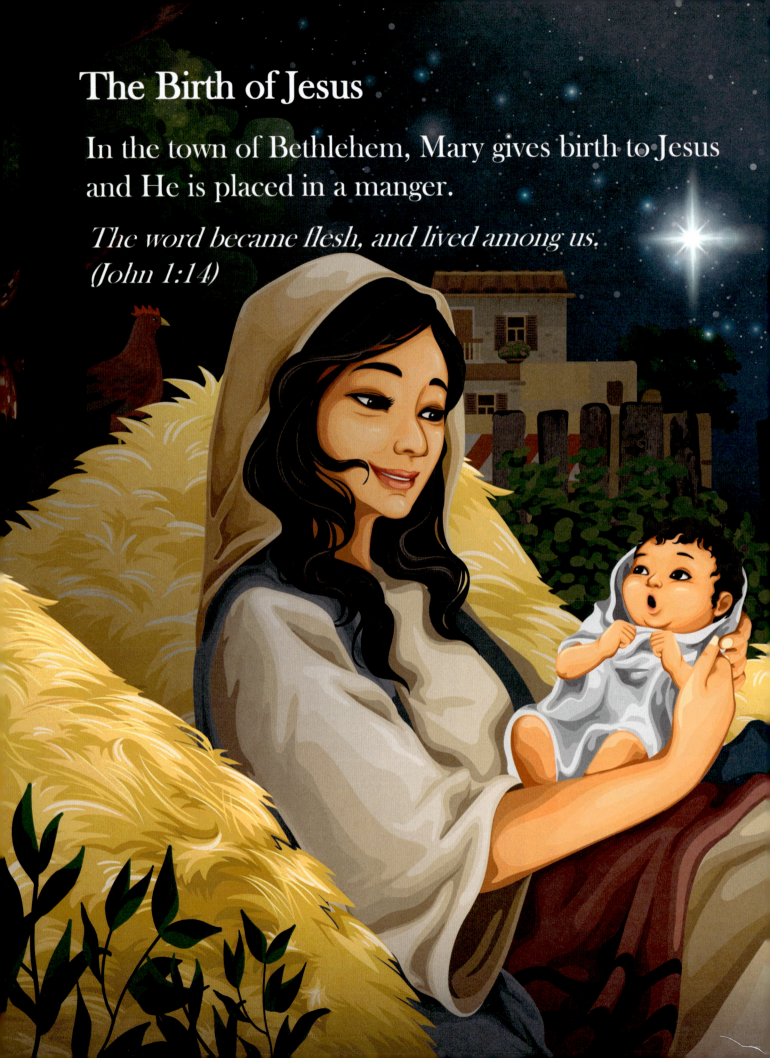

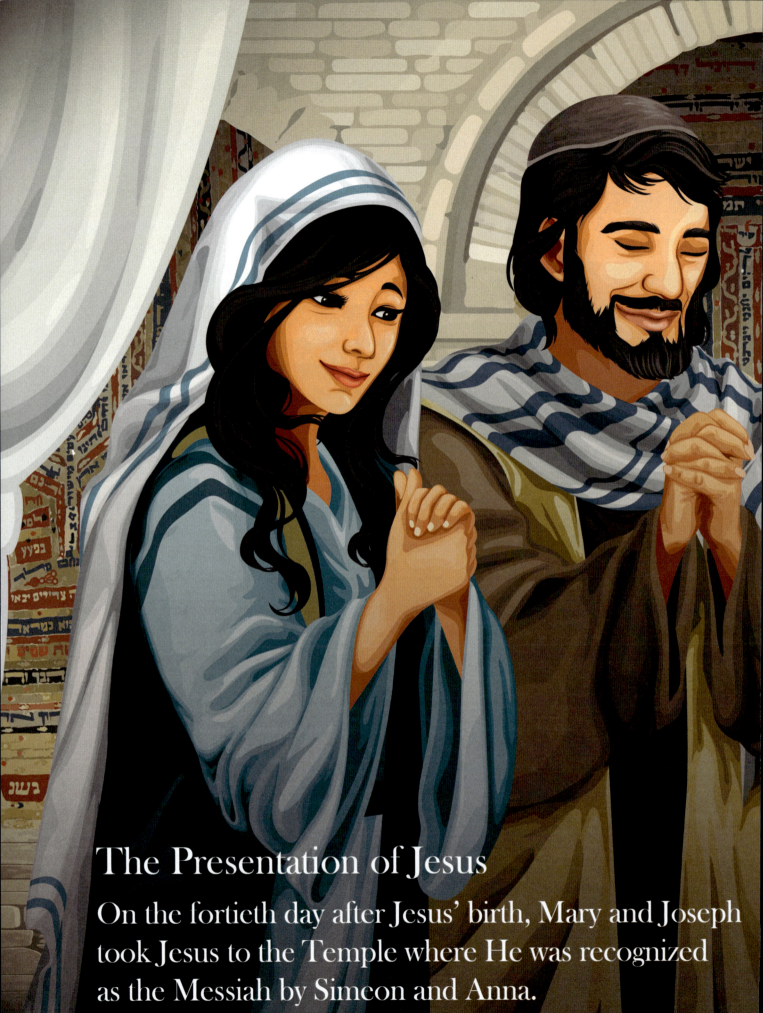

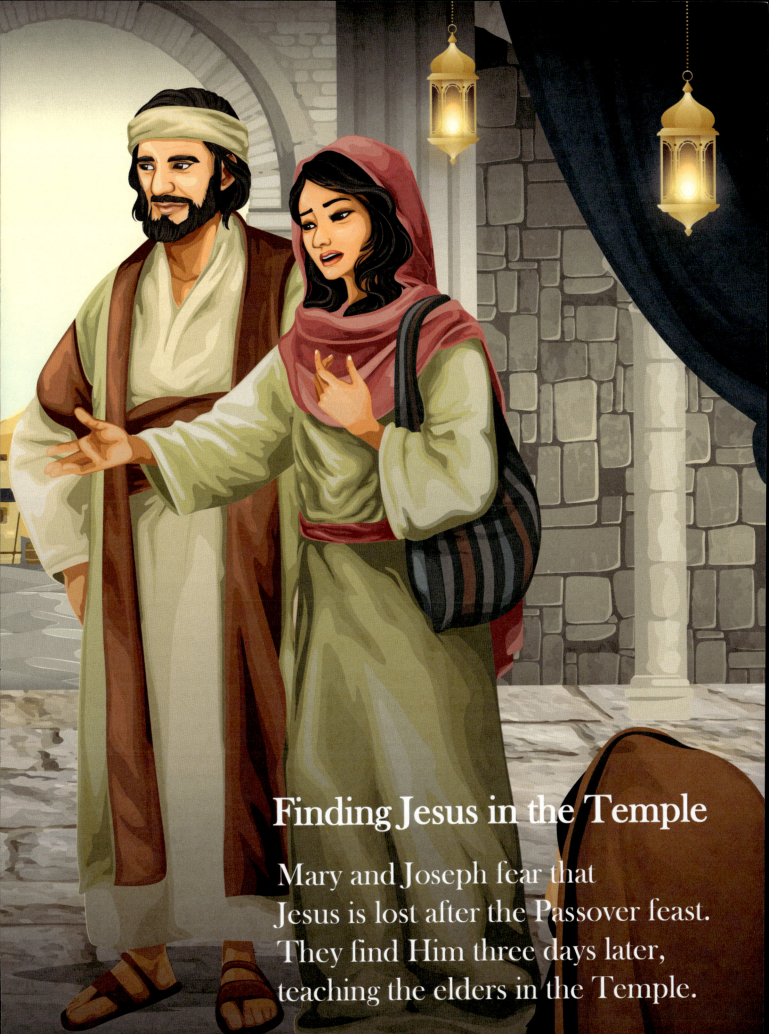

Finding Jesus in the Temple

Mary and Joseph fear that Jesus is lost after the Passover feast. They find Him three days later, teaching the elders in the Temple.

The Luminous Mysteries
(Thursday)

1) The Baptism of Jesus
2) The Wedding Feast at Cana
3) The Proclamation of the Kingdom
4) The Transfiguration
5) The Institution of the Eucharist

The Luminous Mysteries

The Luminous mysteries, also called the Mysteries of Light, show us the Light of God manifested through Jesus.

The Baptism of Jesus

Jesus is baptized by John the Baptist in the Jordan River. After He is baptized, the Spirit of God the Father comes over them like a dove.

A voice says, "This is my beloved Son, with whom I am well pleased."

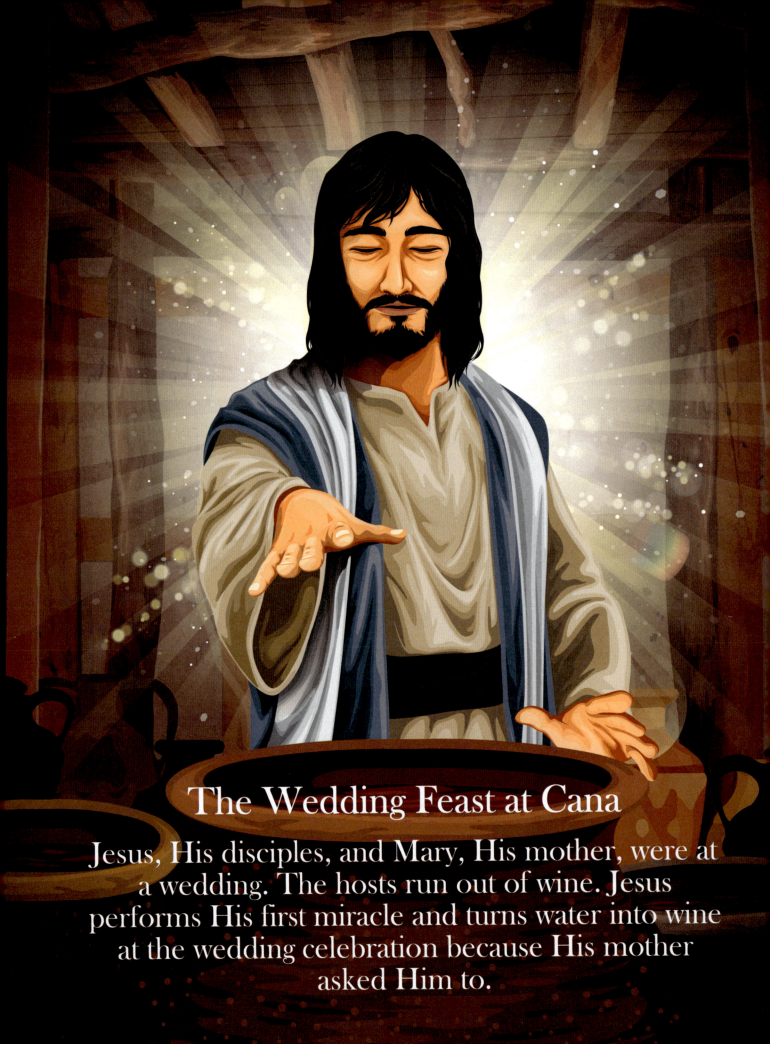

The Wedding Feast at Cana

Jesus, His disciples, and Mary, His mother, were at a wedding. The hosts run out of wine. Jesus performs His first miracle and turns water into wine at the wedding celebration because His mother asked Him to.

The Proclamation of the Kingdom

Jesus tells us about how much God loves us and that we should prepare ourselves for His Kingdom. He asks us to trust God and to love our neighbors as ourselves.

The Transfiguration

Jesus took Peter, James and John up on a mountain where Moses and Elijah appeared. Jesus was transfigured, His face and clothes became bright white.

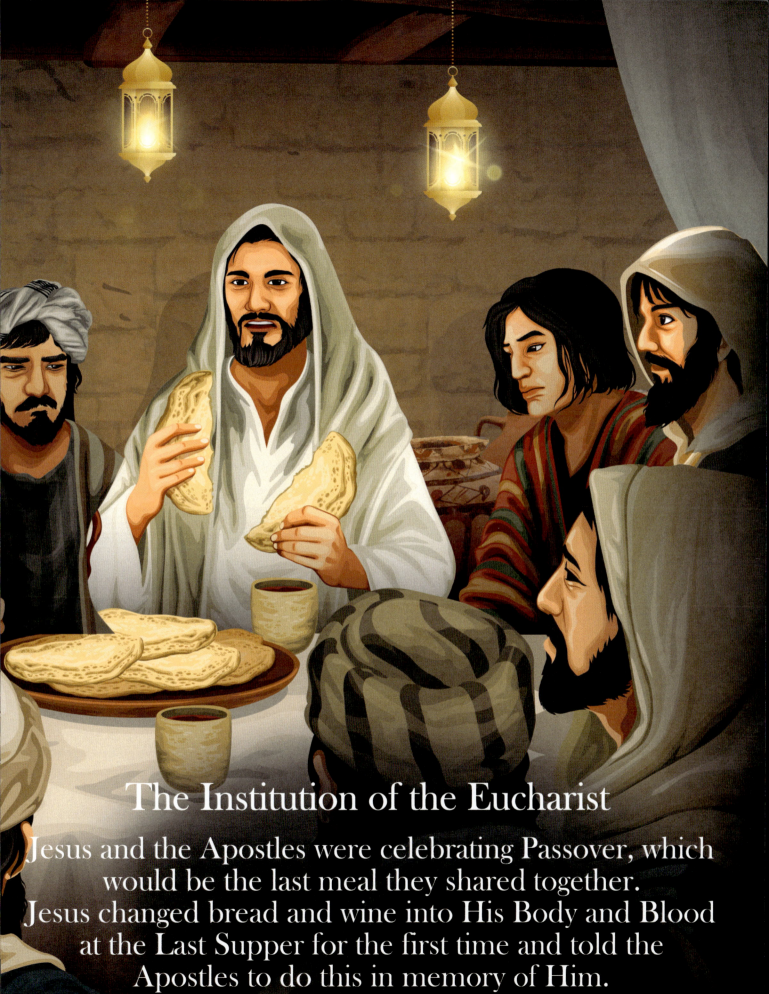

The Sorrowful Mysteries
(Tuesday, Friday and Sundays during Lent)

1) The Agony in the Garden
2) The Scourging at the Pillar
3) The Crowning with Thorns
4) The Carrying of the Cross
5) The Crucifixion

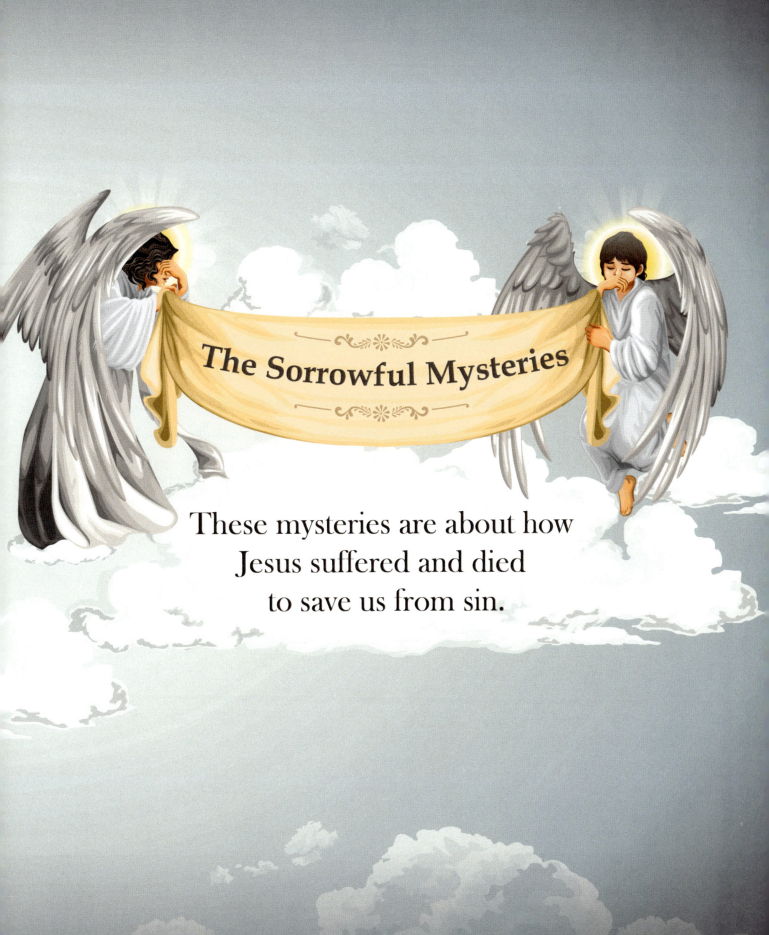

The Sorrowful Mysteries

These mysteries are about how Jesus suffered and died to save us from sin.

The Agony in the Garden

Jesus prays to his Father in the Garden of Gethsemane. He asked his disciples to stay awake and pray but they fell asleep. He asks God, His Father, if He would pass this cup from Him but then says, "Your will be done."

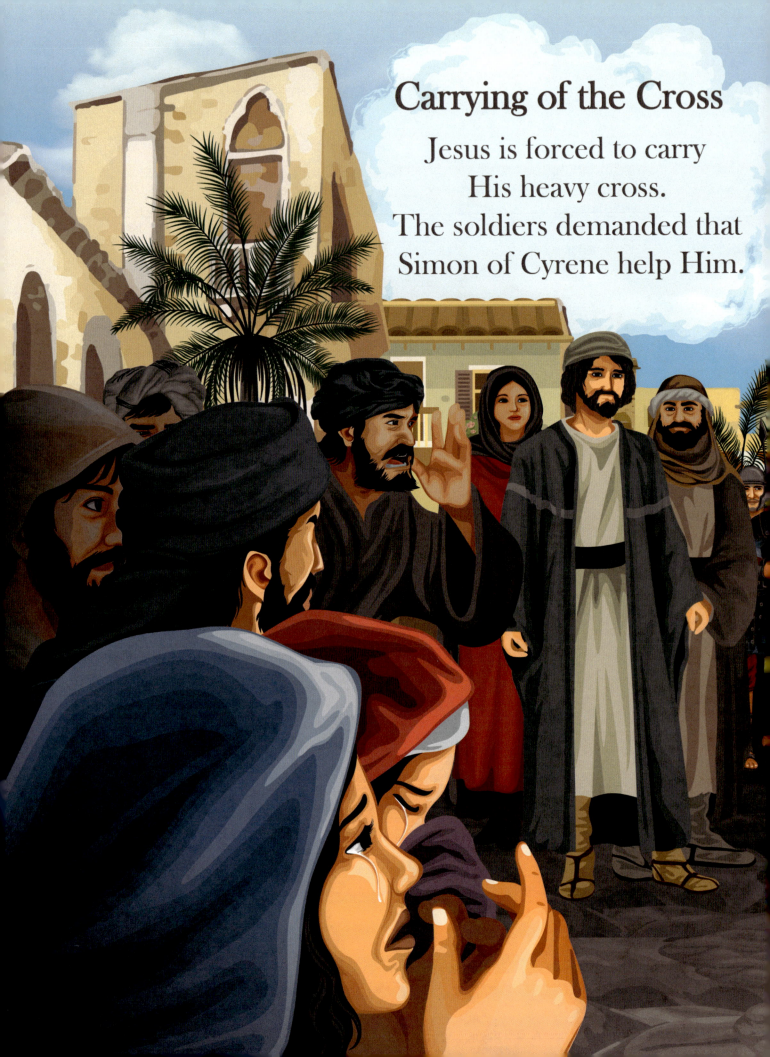

The Crucifixion

Jesus is nailed to the cross.
His mother, Mary and
John the Apostle
watch as He is crucified.

The Glorious Mysteries
(Wednesday and Sunday)

1) The Resurrection of Jesus
2) The Ascension of Jesus into Heaven
3) The Descent of the Holy Spirit
4) The Assumption of Mary into Heaven
5) The Coronation of Mary

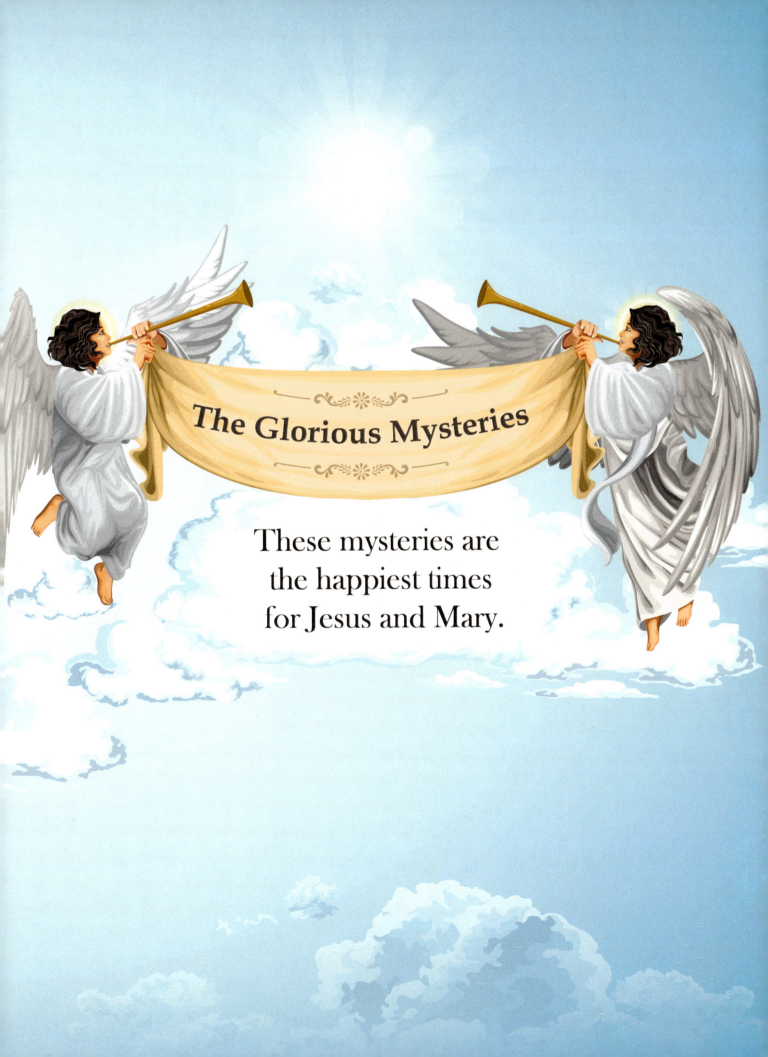

The Glorious Mysteries

These mysteries are the happiest times for Jesus and Mary.

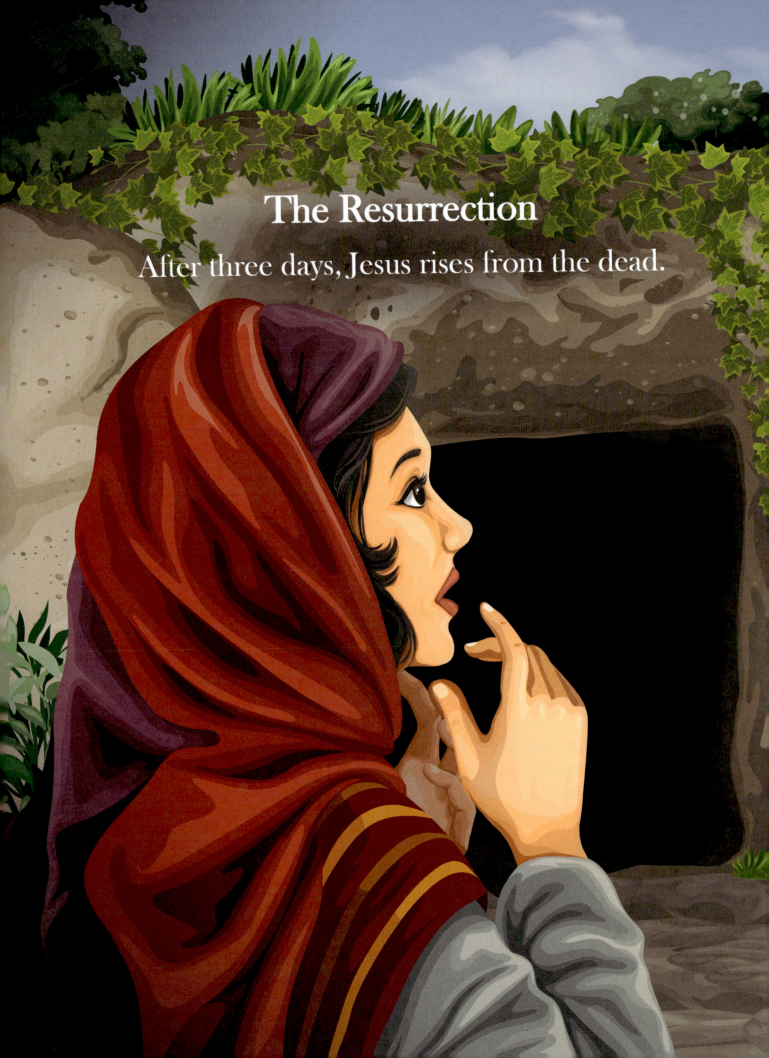

The Resurrection
After three days, Jesus rises from the dead.

The Ascension

Forty days after Jesus rises from the dead,
He ascends body and soul into heaven.

The Assumption

Mary is taken body and soul into heaven to be with her beloved son, Jesus.

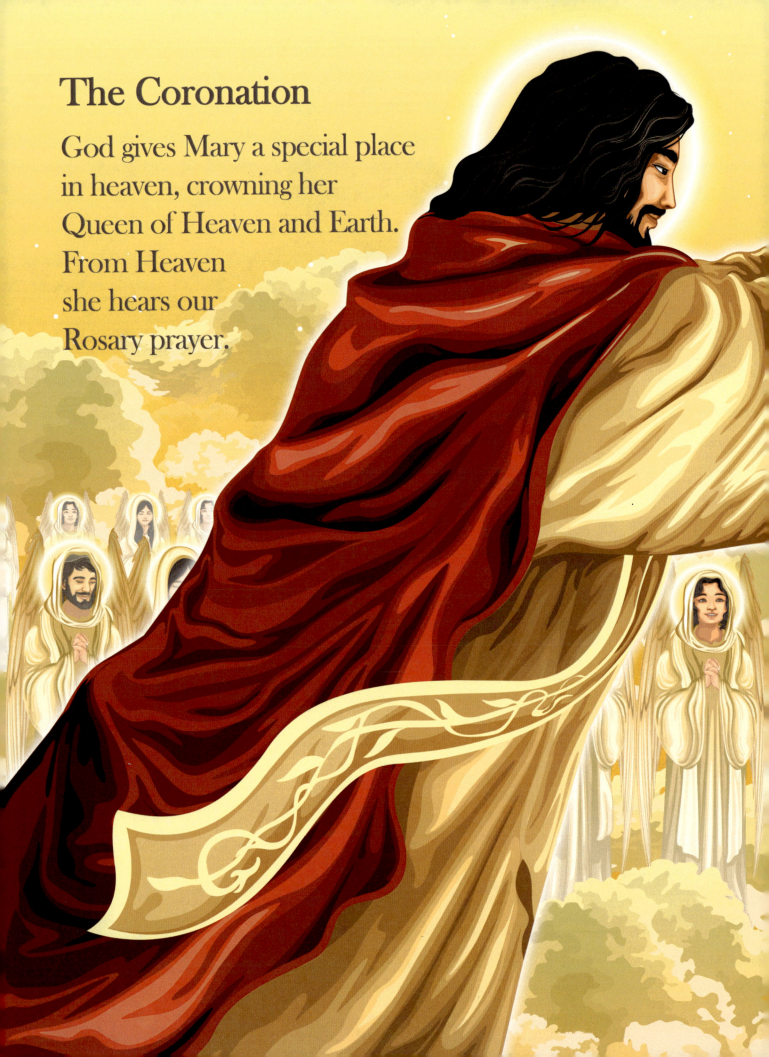

The Coronation

God gives Mary a special place in heaven, crowning her Queen of Heaven and Earth. From Heaven she hears our Rosary prayer.

Made in the USA
Monee, IL
31 October 2023

45497568R00036